D1092870

04463301

PAINT
ME A
POEM

New poems inspired by
paintings and sculptures
in Tate

GRACE NICHOLS

A & C Black • London

For Ruth Kingston

First published 2004 by
A & C Black Publishers Ltd
37 Soho Square, London, W1D 3QZ

www.acblack.com

Text copyright © 2004 Grace Nichols
Page 96 constitutes an extension of this copyright page.

The right of Grace Nichols to be identified as the Author of this work has
been asserted by her in accordance with the
Copyrights, Designs and Patents Act 1988.

ISBN 0 7136 6648 X

A CIP catalogue for this book is available from the British Library.

All rights reserved. No part of this publication may be reproduced in any form
or by any means – graphic, electronic or mechanical, including photocopying,
recording, taping or information storage and retrieval systems – without the
prior permission in writing of the Publishers.

A & C Black uses paper produced with elemental chlorine-free pulp,
harvested from managed, sustainable forests.

Printed and bound in Singapore by Tien Wah Press (Pte) Ltd

LINCOLNSHIRE COUNTY COUNCIL	
04463301	
PETERS	£12.99
02-Oct-2008	821

Contents

Colours that Rhyme

The first poem I wrote about the Tate was 'The Gallery-Ghost'. I liked the idea of an invisible ghost guiding people around the paintings and acting as a kind of supernatural curator when the art gallery is closed at night. I suppose the portraits and staring faces of people long gone can make you feel like that.

But ghost or no ghost, when I was asked by Colin Grigg, Visual Paths Co-ordinator at Tate, to do a year's residency, I was delighted by the invitation because I'd always been intrigued by painting and how poetry and painting have inspired each other. For me, there is a very close relationship between the two art forms. In the compositional balance of a painting, one can almost speak of a certain colour 'rhyming' with a similar colour.

The residency at the Tate involved responding to paintings through poetry as well as working with children from primary schools around London. Some of these children had never visited an art gallery before and their responses to the works were as fresh as their curiosity about the gallery space. Some of the children wrote their poems at the gallery but most continued to work on their poems at school with their teachers.

Even though I've always enjoyed visiting art galleries, my year at the Tate was a new experience for me, as I had to read up about the various artists and familiarise myself with the gallery in general. Learning about the different styles and periods of both painting and sculpture opened up a whole new world for me.

Now, when I look at a painting, I'm more aware of the inner rhythm and harmony of the composition, the play of light and shadow and the whole energy and use of colour. But best of all is simply to forget all of this and become absorbed in the wonder of the work.

6

Gallery-Ghost at the Tate

The Gallery-Ghost is a host with flair,
an art connoisseur who'll show you
which, what and where –
mistress of the art of moving on air.

When she isn't floating
three inches above the gallery floor
to welcome some visitor
through the gallery door

She's gliding down
an Elizabethan corridor
or flitting by Turner
and a reclining Moore.

A friend to all brushstrokes
the Gallery-Ghost
will steer you to what
she wants you to see most.

When you revisit a painting
it's the Gallery-Ghost of course
gently whisking you back in,
because you've missed something.

The Gallery-Ghost,
O the Gallery Ghost
Her dedication puts others to shame.
But whose face is that –
smiling down from an invisible frame?

Grace Nichols

Shape Up With Animals

Brancusi, with his love for the minimal, captures in this piece the very spirit of Bird. Although, in my poem, the bird wants to regain some of its features such as beak and feather, I was captivated by that very featherless symmetry in all its shining elegance.

I was equally intrigued by Matisse's bright cut-out shapes, and felt that there was a snail somewhere in this curving arrangement of colours.

'The Fisheater', on the other hand, has lots of concrete features, unlike both 'Maiastra' and 'The Snail', and makes us think of an actual creature, though weird and no less mysterious.

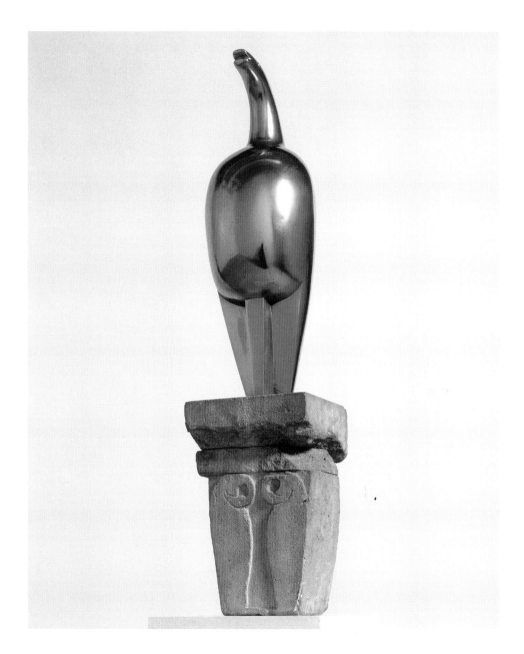

'Maiastra' by Constantin Brancusi

Maiastra

I am the magical bird of dreams
I fly over rivers, oceans and streams.
I stand up straight, but I am old,
That doesn't matter
I still shine like gold.

I will stand up tall and high.
I feel like when I am trapped,
Never reaching the sky.

I am bird of life
I am bird of fire
I am lovely dove
I am the Great Messiah.
I am the Maistra!

Gail
Gloucester Primary

Speak Maistra

Spirit of Bird
Spirit of Fire
Light of the world
I am Maistra
Spilling –
my golden song
like a fountain
over this stone-split.

But feast your eyes and ears, all,
Drink your fill.
For one day I will step out
of my polished perfection –
sprout beak, sprout wings –

On such a day I, Maistra
will leave behind
my gallery grandeur
and get back to the
feathered business of living.

Grace Nichols

Fisheater Chant

Fish for breakfast, lunch and dinner –
watch out fish in stream and river

Fish for brunch and snack and tea –
watch out fish in pool and sea

Mackerel, eel, trout, snapper,
makes no difference to Fisheater.

His taste-buds are rusty –
he's an iron-bird creature

Grace Nichols

'The Fisheater' by Lynn Chadwick

'The Snail' by Henri Matisse

The Snail

Big bright coloured envelopes
in the shape of a snail
but everyone knows
the snail takes no mail
(except perhaps the news of his trail)

Yet this one here with his
big bright coloured envelopes –
Pink
Orange
Yellow
Red
Black
Green

Clearly dreams of being
A postman one day.

Grace Nichols

The Snail

The coloured snail is
    going into the garden
        to eat the green grass.

Reception class
St Gabriel's Church of England

Making Faces

The magnetism of Picasso's 'Weeping Woman' drew me back again and again. The clash of colours, the haggard, fractured features and jagged tears made me think of grief in the widest sense. I was interested to learn that Picasso drew his inspiration for 'Weeping Woman' from the face of Dora Maar, one of the women in his life, and a photographer and artist in her own right. That haunting face made me want to find words to give it a voice.

On the other hand, when I gazed at the portrait of the first Queen Elizabeth, I was struck by the smooth, white oval of her face; both fragile and hard in its mask-like composure. I wrote two poems, one of which was in her own voice. I couldn't help thinking that she would have liked being an Elizabethan adventurer! Perhaps a pirate? Something much more manly than she was allowed to do.

In my poem for 'Marilyn', she reflects on her widely-used image as a Hollywood beauty and sex symbol. Even though she died years ago, her picture is still being used commercially today – some might say exploited – and I suppose the artist is suggesting this by the repetition of her face which becomes more and more faded.

The Queen Who Reigned Supreme

I'd rather be sailing
than sat here being painted,
decked out in this finery,
encrusted with jewellery.

I'd rather be on the high seas
buccaneering the fleets,
taking Spanish galleons,
worth millions and millions.

I'd rather be bandying swords
with the King of Spain.
grappling with his 'Armada'
and singeing his beard.

But I am queen
I reign supreme.

So portraits by common painters
that even in the slightest
rubbish my features,
will be cast in to the fire.

And those who disobey my order
will be shorter – by the head.

Grace Nichols

'Elizabeth I', The Phoenix Portrait
by Nicholas Hilliard

Elizabeth I

No molly-coddler of heads,
you keep yours
a carefully cultivated egg.

Let others lose theirs
to the bloody
towers of history.

Not your icon-lady,
rising out of your
pearl-encrusted dress.

Resting your image
with the chaste
indestructible phoenix, no less.

Uncrackable
despite the red rose
below your breast.

Grace Nichols

Dora Maar (Picasso's Weeping Woman)

They say that instead of a brush
he used a knife on me –
a savage geometry.
But as I say, look again,
this is the closest
anyone has got to the pain.

Green knows me –
Not the green of new shoots,
but the ghastly green of gangrene.
Yellow knows me –
Not the cheery yellow of the sun
but the sickly hues
of this war's putrefaction.
Blue knows me –
Not the boundless blues of sky or sea
but the blues of the singer's
deepest sorrow.

Mother Dolrosa,
this grief has got to me.
Under the poise of my red hat
I hear, as if from a great
distance,
my own stifled scream.

Grace Nichols

'Weeping Woman' by Pablo Picasso

Weeping Woman

I am the woman
with a desolate soul.
I am the woman
whose only son left home.
I am the woman
with diamond bitter tears.
I am the woman
with desperate fears.
I am the woman
without a smile.
I am the woman
with a tragic life.
I am the woman
with coloured hair.
I am the woman
filled with despair.
I am the man she's weeping for.
I am the sky waiting for her.
I am her beloved husband who left her alone.

Nasmin, Foreda, Roison and Shahana
Shapla School

Marilyn

Never mind the airducts
lifting my skirts.
Never mind my giggles
and wiggles and curves.
Never mind my painted toes.

Every flash bulb
was an X-ray
That inched me
Towards the grave.
My whole life an image –
overexposed.

Grace Nichols

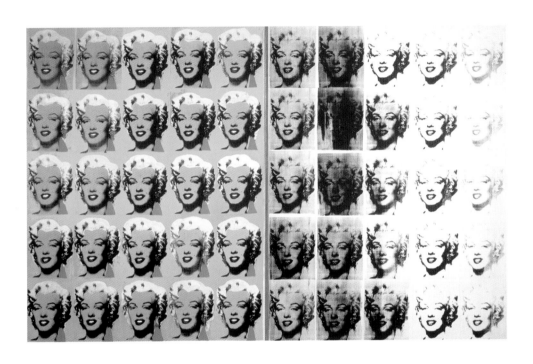

'Marilyn Diptych' by Andy Warhol

Show Me a Story

As a poet, I've always been inspired by legends and mythology. 'The Lady of Shalott' took me back to my own childhood in Guyana, where I first came across Tennyson's poem in an old book of poems. I can still remember the haunting magic of the words that told of a river 'flowing down to Camelot' and the Lady of Shalott. The painting itself has that same, sad, fairytale-like quality.

Another painting that the children enjoyed acting out before they attempted to write their poems was 'Proserpine', also known as 'Persephone', who was snatched to the Underworld by the god Hades. Prosperpine's expression makes me feel that she knows what she is doing, at least in this painting, where she seems to be taking a deliberate bite on that fateful pomegranate.

The women in this section all seem to have suffered a sad fate like that of Shakespeare's tragic character, Ophelia, who drowns in a stream surrounded by plants and wild flowers.

Proserpine Thinks About Her Mother

And when by nightfall I hadn't returned
she set up a wailing on Olympus,

She beat the drums in the assembly places
alerting all the Gods,

She descended to the underworld
bearing her Olympic grief like a torch,

She searched and searched
withdrawing all her energies from earth

She cursed the growing green,
shrivelling wheat and flower

She vowed eternal winter
crying 'Wither, Wither, Wither'

She pulled down heaven, my mother
she pulled up earth, my mother

Because I, her Goddess-daughter, am worth it.

Grace Nichols

'Proserpine'
by Dante Gabriel Rossetti

Proserpine

This is the Pomegranate that made me the prisoner,
the luscious fruit, that keeps me here.
To swallow this fruit, made a dreadful end
in a prison of darkness and fear.

These are the memories I love to dream,
the rippling river and rain,
the rosy smile on my mother's face,
the song of birds at dawn.

This is my life of smiles and tears,
six months here, and six above.
A melancholy dungeon filled with gloom
then a world with a mother's love.

Shahana and Roisin
Shapla School

Ophelia

In a balmy wood
In a balmy brook
Lies a balmy me

Forget-me-not
lying here like an elongated lily
with all my trophies –

Crow-flowers,
nettles, poppies,
willow, pansies, daisies

Hamlet, come no closer
with your 'To be'
I've chosen a brook to marry.

Tell the good queen, your mother,
I may be incapable of my own distress,
but see – I've made a boat of my dress.

Grace Nichols

'Ophelia' by Sir John Everett Millais

The Lady of Shalott

Lady of Shalott,
on a dark, dank day,
on a faraway lake
covered by the dullness of woods.

Lady of Shalott,
fading away on a shabby boat,
praying to God,
and lying down waiting for her ending to happen.

Lady of Shalott,
glassy and sad,
her empty life sailing away,
singing as she lays down, letting go of her chain.

Lady of Shalott,
has passed away,
as she drifts past the king,
Sir Lancelot thought, how did she die?
Not knowing it was he who killed her.

Mathew
Lathom Junior School

Goodbye Shalott

I will not miss you island-tower
I will not miss you days,
seen only through a magic mirror.
My feet have longed to touch
again the grass in summer.

Goodbye Shalott
Goodbye Shalott

When the mirror showed me sweet Lancelot,
my gaze did turn direct upon his features,
for the boldness of this look,
for the bareness of this pleasure,
I am to become Death's Bride – a cold treasure.

Goodbye Shalott
Goodbye Shalott

Down stream I come to meet my lot,
Far away from that
binding mirror.
My heart has always longed
to be as a flowing river.

In a slow boat I come – the Lady of Shalott.
One day I shall break my banks and flood all Camelot.

Grace Nichols

'The Lady of Shalott' by John William Waterhouse

Body Language

Body language speaks deeper than words, and in Degas' 'Little Dancer, Aged Fourteen', you could almost feel the tension of the little dancer and the muscular effort it must take to be a ballet dancer. At the same time, there is a serenity on her face that makes you wonder.

Cezanne's 'Gardener' seems lost in his own contemplation. The overlapping brushstrokes and use of earth colours help to make the gardener at peace with his surroundings in a quiet, mysterious way. And I couldn't help wondering what thoughts were going on under that ochre-coloured hat!

The elongated shapes of Picasso's 'Three Dancers' seem perfectly balanced to me within the painting's composition. But behind the pleasing colours there is a sinister quality to the work.

Little Dancer

Now you must put
your sinewy toes
to their hardest test.

Take a deep breath,
little dancer,
take a deep breath.

Before you burst
into butterfly
from the tight

Cocoon of your dress.

Grace Nichols

Dancer, Dancer

I can see why you are crying,
Dancer,
is it because your feet are burning,
Dancer?
I know you're embarrassed,
Dancer,
But I am impressed
by your dancing,
it is the violins playing sweetly
saying the words,
you know the beats.

Elaina
Gloucester Primary

'Little Dancer Aged Fourteen'
by Edgar Degas

'The Gardener Vallier' by Paul Cezanne

The Gardener

Sitting crossed-legged
under the roof of my hat
hour after hour.

Hearing the leaves
of brushstrokes
overlapping colours.

The workings of greens
and browns and blues
the light over my shoulders.

The patience of seed
the gestures of flowers
my ten green fingers.

Grace Nichols

The Three Dancers

Bending, rocking, twirling
to the invisible strings
of a mad guitar,
played by a mysterious hand –
oblivious to everything but the dance.
Soon, soon, they will take off
bright and dark from the cage
of a balcony into the blue beyond.

Grace Nichols

'The Three Dancers' by Pablo Picasso

Family Values

People like keeping family albums, and looking at some of these paintings was like peering into a family album.

The intimate family moment of a father teaching his daughter to swim ('Melanie and Me Swimming') made me recall watching my own daughter learning to swim.

Not always happy moments like a father and daughter swimming. But also moments of domestic crisis, as in 'The Last Day in the Old Home'. All isn't as it seems. Under all the formality, bankruptcy is going on. The home of a once well-to-do-family is being sold to pay the father's debts, and although he looks cheerful, the painting has a sombre quality.

'The Schutz Family and Their Friends on a Terrace' is about a wedding celebration. The bride's backward glance at her own family seems to suggest a sadness or uncertainty, even as she is stepping into her new life.

Lady Anne

Lady Anne is a silk cushion
On a soft sofa,
A warm scarf in the autumn breeze.

Lady Anne is a warm dusk
With a beautiful sunset,
She is a bee with a caring buzz
And sweet yellow stripes,
A dark red cherry with light brown pip
And dark brown stem.

Lady Anne is a great blue pool
of dark misty water.

Lady Anne is a tear
slowly running down a beautiful cheek,
She is as blue as a broken heart.

Gail
Gloucester Primary

'The Schutz Family and Friends on a Terrace'
by Philip Mercier

Just Married

Now she's sailing forth
from her family's harbour
into the unknown waters
of her husband's life.
A luxury liner, gliding gracefully
towards his seemingly upright family,
she turns the bow of her head
for a last look at her
own familiar shore.

Already her orange-blossom sails
have opened a gulf-stream between them.

Grace Nichols

Last Day in the Old Home

Three cheers to the old house!
Three sneers to the bailiffs!
Wouldn't you say, wife?
But it's been a jolly good life.

The old house has been a brick
Even if a bit too big.
We will miss it
Wouldn't you say, wife?

But we've had some golden times.
What's that, wife,
It's been nothing but lies and strife?
What! Me! Cad? Drink up, lad.

Grace Nichols

'The Last Day in the Old Home'
by Robert Braithwaite Martineau

Wondering WHY?

My father is happy on the outside,
sad on the inside.
All his debts have caught up,
there is nowhere to hide.

I am learning to drink wine.
My dad is acting
as if everything is fine.

My sister is in the corner,
having a little cry,
and I am wondering
WHY?

Sam Leo
Marion Richardson Primary

Learning to Swim
(For Kalera)

Learning to swim,
    your girl-walking
land-accustomed body
turns horizontal wriggly

Arms and legs such strange
    things
like wayward fins
trying to get you from A to B
      to C

And yes you're learning how
    to be
a submarine dancer,
a froggie
a floatie
a spirogyra

Kicking through the new
yet familiar element called
    water.

Grace Nichols

Melanie and Me Swimming

Splish splash went dad
as he was helping Amy to swim

Splish splash went Amy
As she kicked her legs like fins

Splish splash went the
Dark gloomy water

      Splish splash.

Jatin
Vicarage Primary School

'Melanie and Me Swimming' by Michael Andrews

Nature Takes a Turn

I loved Barbara Hepworth's 'Sea Form' with its sea-green, sea-worn smoothness. It was a piece that the children enjoyed working with, and the holes in the sculpture aroused their imagination and a lot of discussion. With its anchor-like weight and shell-like, wave-like curves, it seemed to me like a living artefact of the sea.

Of all the Turner paintings at Tate, I kept being drawn back to his 'Snowstorm – Steamboat off a Harbour's Mouth'. There was something exhilarating about the swirling whirlwind motion of the snowstorm and it was fun to write a poem in the voice of Turner telling-off a critic for saying that his now-famous painting was just a load of soapsuds and whitewash.

Miro's 'Women and Bird in the Moonlight' has an almost child-like quality about it with its simple figures. The whole painting has a soft, incandescant glow that reminds you of the moonlight.

Paula Rego's 'The Dance' has a special magic for me: the faces of the dancers seem both real and unearthly. The different shades of blue and the cobbled cliff and moon contribute to a hauntingly beautiful painting that kept drawing me back.

The bright colours and shapes in Ashile Gorky's abstract painting, 'The Waterfall', made me think of a free-flowing carnival-like figure.

'Snow Storm – Steam-boat off a Harbour's Mouth'
by J M W Turner

Turner to His Critic

(who dismissed his 'Snow Storm – Steam-boat
off a Harbour's Mouth' 1842 as 'soapsuds and
whitewash').
Turner was said to have tied himself to the
mast of a ship to experience a snowstorm.

Soapsuds and whitewash, Critic?
Man, don't make me livid.
I was tied in a snowstorm
to the mast of a ship.
Do you have the foggiest of it?
Do you know what it is to be buffeted?

The buzzard of a blizzard
and the waves churning over me
The wildness of the whirlwind
The horses foaming at my feet

Why, even the sea can see through
her storm-spectacles
that this work is a masterpiece.
Soapsuds and whitewash indeed!
If I had my way, you, Sir, would be
soap-sudded to the bottom of the sea.

Grace Nichols

Waterfall

Water letting
her waterfall-hair down
Waterfall dancing
to her waterfall-sounds
Waterfall dressed-up
every colour under the sun
Waterfall inviting
whistles of bird-call
Waterfall blowing
foamy kisses to one and all

I think Waterfall must be
making her own carnival

Grace Nichols

Magic Waterfall

It is a bizarre day.
All things that I see are
    multi-coloured,
A pool of water,
White mountains of snow frozen,
Green and gold forests of wonder.
A woman bathing under a magical
Waterfall,
Her peachy skin reflects the sun.
She can see a frog with a beard,
A small goat, as tiny as her hand.
Is she dreaming?
Maybe she is under the waterfall
To drown.

Neneh
Gloucester Primary

'Waterfall' by Ashile Gorky

Women and Bird in the Moonlight

I like your Women and Bird
in the Moonlight,
But don't ask me why, Miro,
I just don't know.

Perhaps it's the star
or the bird with a blue tail.
The tilt of those faces
or the magic in the air.

Perhaps it's the colours,
those dots and shapes –
Come together like a poem
on night's glowing face.

I like your Women and Bird
in the Moonlight
But don't ask me why, Miro,
I just don't know.

Grace Nichols

'Women and Bird in the Moonlight' by Joan Miro

Seaform

Seaform, Seaform
from where were you born?

From the ebb and flow
and the eye of the storm

From the lip and lap
and the waves green curl

From the salt and the wind
and all beach movements

I am Porthmeor
the shape of her bewitchment

Grace Nichols

Deep Wave

Deep wave, deep wave
How far have you travelled?
Whoosh

From the bottom of the sea
With the life living in you.
Ssssssshhh … whoosh … psssh.

From the sun and the rain.
You are soft and rough.
Sssssssssshhhhhhhhhhh …

From the eye of the storm
And the waves' green curl.
Pssssh …

From the salt and the wind
How were you born?
Whoooossssssshhhhhhhhh …

You are the King!

Gail
Gloucester Primary

'Sea Form (Porthmeor)' by Barbara Hepworth

'The Dance' by Paula Rego

The Dance

Even the white packed sand
darkened by the shadows
of their dance
is rinsed in blue

Blue nimbus too
over the enigma of faces
the cobbled cliff
the small white moon

Moving to a tune
we'll never know
graceful and solid
in the wind's exposure

How they dance –
these dwellers of the land
Come down to take a stand
against the blue sea

And time that will erase their epitaph

Grace Nichols

When You Look at a Painting

For me the relationship between poems and painting is a close one and each can inspire the other. Both come out of a desire to make something new out of the familiar, to capture an experience in a concentrated way with its own inner rhythm.

In this section I wanted to celebrate some of the elements that go into a painting such as Line, Light, Shape, Balance and Colour – some of the very elements that a poet explores, using words instead of paints.

Line

Holding
form
within
like
a
poem's
building
dark
light
smudged
thick
or
thin –
Van Gogh's
concentric
nerve
tingling
line -
forceful
swirl
of
starry
sky

Light

Breathtaking yellow
of tropical light,
so strong
you could thread
a lizard on it.

Exhilarating gold
of autumn light,
so liquid
you could take
a bath in it.

Shape-revealing
shadow-shifting
colour-bringing light.
All you ask of painting
is to get you right.

Balance

Bringer of aligning grace
Singer of shapes rightly placed.

Shape

O the roundness
posed by a statue's nude buttocks –
and hands, the sneaky shape of hands
reaching out to touch,
despite the gallery attendant's
reprimanding glance –

Our instinct for curves
The fine smooth grain of things.

Grace Nichols

Colour Reunion

Brother Green, so highly esteemed,
wipes his face in his leafy sleeves.

Sister Yellow, with a burst of laughter,
strokes the canary on her shoulder.

Uncle White stands at the window
remembering his small days in the snow.

Auntie Blue in her satiny cerulean
rolls in like a wave off the Mediterranean.

Father Red, a flaming hat on his head,
strolls in looking devilishly dread.

Mother Black with winkling eye
spreads her starry tablecloth from on high.

'Grandpa Brown and Grandma Purple
Greatuncle Grey and Greataunt Silver.

'Not to mention Cousins Mauve and Magenta
They're all coming, yes all coming to dinner.'

Grace Nichols

When You Look at a Painting

When you look at a painting
let the dancing begin.
Move your eyes round the frame
both gilded and plain.
Then let the light take you in
To all that's within.

When you look at a painting
just don't stand and stare.
Slide your eyes round the waists
of the colours and the shades,
let your eyes keep step
with the moods and the shapes.

When you look at a painting
let the dancing begin.
Let the rhythm unlock
the way your body rocks.
Don't be shy, let your eyes jump in –
Surprise the dancefloor of the painting.

Grace Nichols

About the Art

by Colin Grigg, Co-ordinator, Visual Paths at Tate

'Maiastra' (1911) by Constantin Brancusi (1876–1957)

Brancusi is one of the most important modern sculptors, yet he was born into a family of peasant farmers in a remote village in Romania. In 1904, determined to travel to Paris to study sculpture but penniless, he had to walk most of the thousand miles. French sculpture was then dominated by the realism of Rodin ('The Kiss'), but Brancusi wanted to capture the essence of things, not their outward appearance. He stripped away the details and complexity to arrive at bold simple forms.

This sculpture is inspired by a Romanian folk story. In the story the hero seeking his true love, a princess, is guided through a dark forest by the song of a magical bird who leads him to where she is imprisoned.

'The Fisheater' (1951) by Lynn Chadwick (1914-2003)

Lynn Chadwick was born in London and trained in engineering and architecture. During the Second World War he was a pilot with the Fleet Air Arm. He became a designer for exhibition displays, and as part of this produced mobiles which he later developed into sculptures.

A mobile is a sculpture that uses hanging forms that turn in the wind to give ever-changing arrangements of shapes and planes. These works are constructed, rather than carved or modelled, using techniques from engineering such as welding, cutting and forming sheet metal.

'Fisheater' was made for the 1951 Festival of Britain, to celebrate a new vitality in British industry after the austerity of the war years. 'Fisheater' has a spiky menacing quality that an art critic called 'the geometry of fear' that harks back to the fear and violence of the war.

'The Snail' (1953) by Henri Matisse (1869–1954)

Matisse was born in 1869 in the North of France, but it was the dazzling colours and sunlight of Southern France that made him the extraordinary modern artist he became. Matisse was above all a colourist and he often compared colours to music.

In 1941, aged 72, Matisse underwent a serious operation for stomach cancer that left him wheelchair-bound for the rest of his life. Undeterred, he sought new ways of working. His assistants would cover huge sheets of paper with pure colours of gouache. Matisse would then take a large pair of scissors and cut out shapes. He called it, "cutting into colour". It reminds me of a sculptor's direct carving. The snail was one of the last of these works and, at nearly three metres square, includes the largest cut-outs Matisse ever made.

'Elizabeth I, The Phoenix Portrait' (1576) by Nicholas Hilliard (1546-1618)

Hilliard became an artist/craftsman to Queen Elizabeth I. The Queen, like modern day celebrities, was concerned to control her image and at one time had over six hundred inferior images of herself confiscated and burnt. She turned to Nicholas Hilliard to create her portrait, not only to be a great work in its own right, but also to serve as a model for other painters to follow.

Portrait-painting involves three roles: the artist, the sitter and the person who pays for the work. Whoever pays controls how the portrait is made. In this case, the Queen was both the sitter and the one who paid. Queen Elizabeth was a vain, powerful woman and she wanted a decidedly flattering and regal portrait.

'Weeping Woman' (1937) by Pablo Picasso (1881–1973)

Picasso was the most famous artist in the world of the twentieth century. Picasso is equally famous for the many beautiful women he loved. With each new romance there was a change of style in his work. As well as a painter he was an extraordinary sculptor, printmaker and potter.

In 1937 the fascist general Franco led a military takeover in Picasso's native Spain. Picasso was living in Paris but wanted to show his opposition to fascism so he painted a large, powerful mural. This was his greatest work and is known simply as 'Guernica'. The painting features a woman crying, and Picasso continued this theme after completing the mural. 'Weeping Woman' is part of that series. Dora Maar, a Yugoslavian photographer, was the model for this intense expression of grief.

'Marilyn Diptych' (1962) by Warhol (1928–1987)

'Publicity is like peanuts. Once you start you can't stop,' Warhol once said. He was a successful commercial illustrator before he became an artist. He created glossy advertisements and shop window displays – many around fashion items such as women's shoes. His own life and the images he produced were concerned not with real people, but with the mask of celebrity.

In 1962 the screen goddess Marilyn Monroe died. Television coverage around the world showed images of her again and again, reducing her tragic death to numbing repetition. Soon after the event, Andy Warhol began a large series of works based on a single 'glamour' image from the film Niagara. In the Marilyn Diptych, the artist shows us this gaudy plastic face on the left and contrasts it with the smudged, black funeral image on the right. The images make us aware, much as we were made aware with Princess Diana, that the media can not only make but also destroy a celebrity.

'Proserpine' (1874) by Dante Gabriel Rossetti (1828–1882)

Rossetti was a poet as well as painter, and the energetic leader of the Pre-Raphaelite Brotherhood that sought to return to the richness and symbolism of mediaeval art and legends.

The story of Proserpine is of a beautiful girl kidnapped by Pluto, the king of the underworld. He drags her off in his chariot to the land of the dead where he marries her against her will. Proserpine's mother, Ceres, pleads with the gods for her release, who agree providing she has not eaten the food of the dead. Alas starving Proserpine nibbles a few seeds from a pomegranate which Pluto has tempted her with. So it is decided she must spend six months above ground each year and six months below ground.

'Ophelia' (1852) by Sir John Everett Millais (1829–1896)

Millais, like Picasso, was a boy genius. He was the youngest person ever to enter the Royal Academy Schools, at the age of eleven. He went on to pass all the exams and win all the painting prizes. Millais was an enormously successful artist and he sold this work to the sugar manufacturer Henry Tate for £3,000 – equivalent perhaps to over £100,000 today. Later, Henry Tate gave money for the building of the Tate gallery at Millbank and donated this painting to the collection.

Ophelia is an innocent woman who dies for love and was a favourite theme for the Pre-Raphaelites. A character from Shakespeare's Hamlet, Ophelia is driven mad when her lover, Hamlet, murders her beloved father. She drowns in a stream clutching a garland of wild flowers and herbs.

'The Lady of Shalott' (1888) John William Waterhouse (1849–1917)

Waterhouse was born in Rome, where his father was a painter. He studied under his father until he entered the Royal Academy in 1870. In 1886 he saw an exhibition of Millais paintings and was inspired to produce works with a similar Pre-Raphaelite theme, to which he brought a classical training and dream-like mood. As a child he had enjoyed myths and legends and these now inspired his work.

Alfred, Lord Tennyson was a very popular poet and the Lady of Shalott proved a great success. Waterhouse painted three different scenes from the story. The poem is set in the legendary time of King Arthur. The beautiful Lady of Shalott is under a mysterious curse that forbids her to gaze on real life. She lives alone, imprisoned, only able to observe the world as reflected in a mirror. In this way she represents the restricted lives of many middle and upper class women in Victorian society. She spends her days singing and weaving a tapestry of the scenes she sees reflected in the mirror. In this scene she has escaped the tower but the curse is upon her.

'Little Dancer Aged Fourteen' (1906) by Edgar Degas (1834 – 1917)

Degas was born and lived in Paris. His father wanted his son to be a lawyer, but though Edgar registered for a law degree he spent most of his time drawing old masters in the Louvre. Degas was influential in organising the Impressionist exhibitions where he exhibited along with artists such as Monet, Cezanne and Renoir. Degas had begun by painting the theatrical glitter of a ballet performance, but later he came to record the less glamorous hard work that went on backstage.

Though Degas made sculptures all his life, 'Little Dancer' was the only one he exhibited. After his death over 150 clay and wax sculptures were found in his studio. Some seventy of these, including 'Little Dancer' were subsequently cast in bronze by Albert Bartholme.

'The Gardener Vallier' (1906) by Paul Cezanne (1839–1906)

Paul Cezanne was born, and lived most of his life in Aix-en-Provence in the South of France. He lived a quiet, ordered life but his art was revolutionary. Becoming an artist was a long struggle for the young Cezanne, whose early work was dark and awkward, but through friendship with Pissarro, he began to use a lighter, brighter range of colours. He showed with the Impressionists and, like them, believed in working directly from nature. However his approach was not concerned with the transitory sensations of light so much as with wanting to 'make of Impressionism something solid and lasting like the art of museums'. In the last years of his life, Cezanne had a studio some miles out of town on a hill overlooking Aix-en-Provence. Vallier tended the garden around the studio and became a model for a series of paintings. Cezanne was probably working on this painting when he was taken ill and died.

'The Three Dancers' (1925) by Pablo Picasso (1881–1973)

This painting is one of the great masterpieces in the Tate collection, but it began as something very different. Picasso started this large painting as a classical picture of three dancers or the three 'graces', but during the painting he received news of an old friend's death that turned these angelic maids of the goddess of love into three writhing monsters.

Picasso suggests that women are two-faced by incorporating a second, crescent moon face in the left-hand head. This face is gentler, but the overall feeling of the composition is one of frenzy. If the original three graces had suggested classical ballet music, the finished work, with its harsh colours and jagged forms, suggests heavy metal rock.

'In the old days pictures went forward to completion by stages. Every day brought something new. A picture used to be a sum of additions. In my case a picture is a sum of destructions. I do a picture – then destroy it. In the end, though, nothing is lost; the red I took away from one place turns up somewhere else' (Picasso).

'The Shutz Family and Friends on a Terrace' (1725) by Philip Mercier (1689–1760)

Mercier was born in Germany of French parents but spent most of his adult life in England. He earned his living painting local gentry in Yorkshire in a 'French manner'. His artistic influences were the French artists, Chardin and Watteau and he may have supplemented his income by painting fake Watteau's.

The Shutz family, who presumably commissioned this painting, were well connected in the Hanoverian court and accompanied George II to England. The orange tree on the right is a symbol of marriage and indicates this is a painting that celebrates the marriage of the son and heir to the beautiful young country girl shown in the centre.

The artist captures the moment when the girl, rather like Melanie in the Michael Andrews painting, is leaving the protection of her own family and taking a step into her new husband's unfamiliar world.

She looks back with nostalgia at her past and goes forward with apprehension. And well she might as the collection of people on the right seem a strange unfriendly bunch, particularly the severe looking mother-in-law.

In the background is the estate of her new family. A fine horse is prepared – perhaps as a wedding gift to her. This is a painting that seals a contract perhaps between a farming family and the aristocratic Shutz family – a contract as much about wealth and possessions as about love.

'The Last Day in the Old Home' (1862) by Robert Braithwaite Martineau (1826–1869)

Many Victorians believed art should tell stories and have a moral message. Indeed some believed art could change people's lives. In this painting, Martineau is preaching the evils of gambling.

The scene is set in the family home of a good-for-nothing cad who has gambled away the family fortune. The betting book, dice and racing picture on its side suggest where the money has gone. The picture frame is decorated with a victor's laurel and a jester's cap and bells with the dates 1523 and 1860, symbolising the fall of the family. The house and all its contents are to be sold to pay his debts. The grandmother is handing over the deeds to a lawyer but the husband shows no remorse as still clutching some cards, he introduces his son to drinking wine. The wife, worn weary with worry sits sadly, whilst her daughter, gently clutching a doll, gazes at her mother's altar on the sideboard.

'Melanie and Me Swimming' (1979) by Michael Andrews (1928–1995)

Michael Andrews became identified with the 'School of London' in the 1960s. This was a group of friends who championed figurative art at a time when abstract art was all the rage. Their work was largely concerned with recording people and places they knew, much as Degas had done in Paris a century before.

During the 1970s, Andrews, his wife and daughter, spent summer holidays in Scotland, and it was there a friend photographed him teaching his daughter to swim. Andrews used these photographs as a starting point for the painting. Melanie had also recently started school and so was experiencing that dramatic moment of setting out into the wider world. The artist reflects this in the way he is shown both supporting her efforts, yet encouraging her to swim free. His face is turned way so that we experience the event only through Melanie's expression of terror and excitement.

'Snow Storm – Steam-boat off a Harbour's Mouth' (1842) by J.M.W. Turner (1775–1851)

Turner's early works were careful studies of great buildings and picturesque landscapes in watercolours, but as his ability and success grew he began to explore the dramatic, atmospheric aspects of nature. Along with the great poets of his time such as Wordsworth and Byron, he became interested in the grandeur and power of nature, in particular the changing moods of the sky and sea.

Turner was in his sixties when he painted a steam-boat caught in a snow storm yet he claimed to have actually experienced this first-hand. This is probably an old fisherman's tale but what is not in doubt is Turner's ability to suggest the terrors of being in a small boat in the middle of a storm. When Turner exhibited this painting at the Royal Academy some of the critics were very unkind, labelling it 'soapsuds'.

'Waterfall' (1943) by Ashile Gorky (1904–1948)

Gorky was born in Armenia, when it was occupied by Turkey. At fifteen, he and his younger sister fled Armenia, arriving as refugees at Ellis Island New York. He became a major American modern artist, yet his art remained ingrained with memories of his mother and his childhood in Armenia.

His art went through many changes, first influenced by Cezanne, then Picasso and in his later years by Miro. 'Waterfall' may have been inspired by a souvenir postcard of a couple embracing in a wood against a background of Niagara Falls. It marks the beginning of his most important period of work that culminated, at the age of 44, in his hanging himself in a barn. This followed a fire that had destroyed many of his greatest works and a car accident that left his painting arm paralysed.

'Women and Bird in the Moonlight' (1949) by Joan Miro (1893–1983)

Miro was born in Catalonia, Spain. His life changed when he met the Surrealist writers and artists in Paris in 1920. Andre Breton, leader of the Surrealist Movement, described it in these terms: 'I believe in the future resolution of these two states … which are dreams and reality, a sort of absolute reality, or surreality.'

Of his work, Miro said, 'Rather than setting out to paint something, I begin painting and as I paint, the picture begins to assert itself, or suggest itself under my brush. The form becomes a sign for a woman or bird as I work.' Following this free, doodling session, he would become more controlled in developing the images. 'To me it seems vital that a rich and robust theme should be present to give the spectator an immediate blow between the eyes.'

'Sea Form (Porthmeor)' (1958) by Barbara Hepworth (1903–1975)

Barbara Hepworth was the first great British woman sculptor. It was a slide show of Egyptian art given by her teacher when Barbara was seven that awakened her interest in sculpture.

With the outbreak of the Second World War, Hepworth and her husband, the painter Ben Nicholson moved ith their children to St Ives, Cornwall. The Cornish landscape became an inspiration for her work for the rest of her life. Hepworth began as a carver in wood and stone, but in 1956 she began having works cast in bronze. 'Sea Form' was first made by building up plaster over an aluminium armature. The plaster was then carved to create the finished surface, before being cast into bronze. The finished cast was then treated with chemicals to produce the rich range of colours we see today.

'The Dance' (1988) by Paula Rego (b 1935)

Paula Rego was born in Portugal in 1935. For her first few years she lived with her grandmother, in a house in Lisbon, where she was very happy. But when she went to live with her parents, on the coast at Estoril, she says, 'I was afraid of everything.'

Rego's art is strongly narrative, recalling childhood memories, fears and fantasies. These 'stories' draw heavily on nursery rhymes and folk tales told to her by her grandmother and aunt, as well as taken from newspapers, films and personal occurrences in her life. Her paintings frequently feature strong women and stern girls who bring a disturbing note to mundane household tasks, like feeding a dog or polishing boots.

'The Dance' is set on a beach in Portugal. It is a festival from her own childhood transformed into an allegory of a woman's life from childhood to old age.

Get Inspired!

by Colin Grigg, Co-ordinator, Visual Paths at Tate

If you have enjoyed reading the poems that Grace and the children created from works of art maybe you would like to have a go yourself? All you need to get started is a love and curiosity for words: the sounds they make, the way they can paint pictures in our heads, the way they can dance and sing.

Long before there were poetry books, people enjoyed poetry through chants and songs that were passed on from generation to generation. Think of playground nursery rhymes such as 'Old King Cole' and 'Ring a Ring a Roses'. These are hundreds of years old, yet we still chant them today. We love them because they have a strong rhythm and speak of curious things. You may have started being a poet by inventing your own verses to such nursery rhymes.

The best way to begin is by reading and listening to lots of poems, rhymes and songs. Try to work out what it is you like about your favourite ones. If you have a favourite pop song, write down the words and explore how they fit the music. Music has a beat, often marked by the drum or bass guitar in pop music. Poems also have a beat and rhythm and this is what makes Grace Nichols' poems so memorable.

Tips for Writing Poetry

1 A poem has to grow like a plant. Begin with a seed: a few words, a phrase or a theme, then nurture it. It may grow quickly or take months before it is fully formed and flowers into a stunning new poem.

2 Keep a notebook and pencil handy at all times, so you can jot things down immediately you see or experience something interesting, or a marvellous phrase occurs to you. The seeds of poems can appear anywhere – on a bus, playing football or as you drift into sleep. You need to jot them down straight away to capture the energy and magic.

3 Only write about things that excite or interest you, so they have something to excite and interest the reader.

4 When something captures your interest, write it down as you think it or say it. Don't try to create a poem straight away. Focus on the subject; cut yourself off from other distractions. Just scribble notes, words or sentences in whatever form is convenient. Some people like to write it out like a story.

5 Try to capture the experience using all five senses: smell, touch, taste, hearing as well as sight. This helps the reader to feel part of the scene.

6 Once you have collected lots and lots of jottings you can start to sift through them all and find the general shape of a poem. Highlight strong words and phrases; get rid of vague and general phrases. Look for vivid descriptions and lively action words. Don't be afraid to look in a dictionary and thesaurus to enrich your writing.

7 Don't try to force rhymes it can destroy what you're trying to say, but do look for strong rhythms. Keep reading out loud what you have written so you can judge its effect and clarity.

8 To test how your poem is going, get a friend to read it out loud. Do they convey the feelings and meaning and do they follow the rhythm as you meant it to be? If not, where are the awkward or confusing words? How can you write the poem to read more effectively?

9 Be bold. Never be afraid to make changes, not only to words but to the order of the lines. Sometimes a line near the top can go better at the end, or a line near the end can go better near the beginning.

10 Above all, however long it takes to write, a poem when finished needs to come alive for the reader, to feel fresh and unexpected.

Speaking Pictures

When working from a work of art or other visual objects the following sequence might be helpful.

Observation

Begin by taking a long, careful look at the whole work of art you have chosen. Let it speak to you in all its richness and variety. Now staying with what you can actually see, make sketches of the overall composition and of details that interest you. Pick out the one telling detail that conveys the feeling or idea you want to write about.

Turn away from the artwork and try to remember as much as you can of it. Jot down what you can remember. Now turn back to look at it and describe it in all its particular detail. You might start by listing things, such as the objects and colours in a painting. Then take each one and go on to describe it in more detail.

Try to find words and phrases that accurately reveal the qualities of the work that interest you.

Experience

Once you have described what you can see, reflect on how this relates to your own life and things you have personally experienced. This will help you give life and depth to what you write.

For example, if there is a bird that sings outside your window in summer, think of the joy it brings you and the music it makes when you write about the magic 'Maiastra' bird. Or if you have felt like a small fish at the mercy of a big 'Fisheater', such as when a bully has picked on you, then that will help you write about that sculpture. Or a colour in a painting may attract you because it reminds you of something you love. For example, as the orange shape in Matisse's 'Snail' may remind you of the colour of a favourite dress or T-shirt.

Imagination

The artwork can only be experienced visually, but you can imagine what sounds, smells, taste and textures it might have. Can you imagine, what it would be like if it came alive? What would happen if you could enter the painting? What might happen next?

Meaning

Finally, think what it might mean – for you and for the artist. What motivated the artist to make it? What symbols are there and what might they mean?

Poem Building

All the above can come into your jottings about a work of art. From this long list you can then begin to select what you want to put in the poem and what form the poem will take. Let the work and your ideas lead you. A simple, stark object like the sculpture "Maiastra" may need a simple stark poem, whilst the complicated set of shapes and balances in Fisheater may need a more complicated poem.

'As' you 'like' it

One of the things that marks poetry out from other forms of writing is the colourful language – helped by the use of similes and metaphors.

When you want to describe an object or experience to another person you might compare it to something else that conveys the particular quality you want to emphasise. For example, a man with a deep booming voice might be described as having a voice like a foghorn. Or a girl who is shy and quiet may be described as being as quiet as a mouse. These are similes, or phrases that suggest one thing is like something else. We usually link an object to its simile by using the words 'as' or 'like'.

Grace Nichols uses similes in many of her poems. In 'Learning to Swim', she compares learning to swim to being:

> A submarine dancer
> A froggie
> A floatie
> A spirogyra

Let's look at the father in the painting 'Last Day in the Old Home'. What kind of expression does he have? You might say he has a grin like a snake or a fox.

You can now extend the description by asking questions of the simile: How do snake's grin? Or, why would a fox grin? A snake's grin is ruthless and full of poison. A fox grins when it is about to pounce on its prey.

If we put it all together we can begin to get a very rich description:

The father grinned like a snake, ruthless and full of poison.

See how by linking the two images together we have started to create something exciting. Now you can take other things in the painting and do the same for them.

Magic Metaphor

Whilst a simile suggests one thing is like another, metaphor suggests one thing has magically transformed into another. So instead of saying, 'The big man was like a bear', you can say, 'He was a bear of a man.'

We can turn any simile into a metaphor and make our imagery even stronger. The father's expression in 'Last Day in the Old Home' could become, 'His ruthless snake-grin was full of poison.'

Syllable

There is just one more thing to explain before we get into the poetry games syllables. Syllables are like the notes in music and help give a line of poetry its musical quality. You need to speak the word out loud to hear how many syllables it has. The word 'red' is a one-syllable word, whilst the word 'winter' is two – 'win' and 'ter'. The word 'hospital' has three – 'hos', 'pit' and 'al'.

Poetry Games

by Colin Grigg, Co-ordinator, Visual Paths at Tate

Begin by choosing a painting or sculpture that interests you. In each section I will suggest artworks you could work with, but do feel free to choose others.

Kennings

These are an ancient Norse way of describing something by linking pairs of its characteristics. So a pair of scissors becomes a hair-cropper, or a paper-snipper, or more interestingly, a nail-trimmer.

Take an object from one of the works of art, such as the golden bird, or the brightly-coloured snail and try to make your own list of kennings. They can make great riddles:

> He's steel-legged
> With sharp toes
> A hair-cropper
> Whether open or closed
> A nail-trimmer
> And a paper-snipper
> So don't go
> Crossing swords with him.

Let's Make Haiku

Haiku is a form of poem that came originally from Japan. One traditional form comprises just three lines with five, then seven, then five syllables. This small poem is best used to capture a detail or single sensation. You need to choose your words very carefully, so each conveys as much meaning as possible.

> Bright star flickering
> Behind the dazzling gold mask
> Cold night approaches.
> ('Marilyn Diptych' by Andy Warhol)

A variation on the haiku is the lune. This is a three line poem with three, then five, then three words.

> Out of sight
> Young girl suffers to become
> Tomorrow's perfect dancer.
> ('The Young Dancer' by Edward Degas)

Acrostic Poems

In an acrostic poem a keyword is written vertically down the page and the poem is formed by using the letters to start each line. Try using the title of an artwork. Here is an acrostic to Barbara Hepworth's sculpture 'Sea Form'.

> **S**ee how the waves
> **E**ndlessly curl
> **A**fter the shore.
>
> **F**ish gently swirl
> **O**ver the spray
> **R**acing the tide
> **M**aking for shore.

Watching the Detectives

Detectives closely observe the scene of a crime to gather evidence and clues. Once they have this information they can begin to suggest what it means. We can do the same with a work of art. Begin by closely looking at all the details: the setting, the time of day, the figures, their clothes, pose, expression, and so on. Use these details to suggest what might be going on in the painting.

Write one line of close description then a line of interpretation. You can continue like this until a whole painting and story emerges (the hill in the background of Paula Rego's 'The Dance').

> A dark mountain full of caves
> Where pirates hide their gold
> On moonlit nights.

The Secret Life of Objects

Choose an animal or object from a painting. It could be the red wig in the portrait of Queen Elizabeth or the thornless rose she is holding. Whatever you choose, imagine it could think. What sort of character would it be? Now tell the story of the painting as seen by that object or animal. You can turn it into a chant by beginning each verse like this:

> I am the owl that …
> I am the rose that …

The Furniture Game

This activity is based on Sandy Brownjohn's excellent book 'Does it Have to Rhyme?' Gail's poem 'Lady Anne' was created using this game. Look closely at the painting and see how Gail has interpreted the woman in the centre. Now choose a character from one of the paintings and ask yourself: if this person was a piece of furniture what would it be? Then ask the question: what kind of weather? What music? What colour? What animal? What place? What season? and so on. The list is endless.

Questions and Answers

It is good to do this in pairs. Choose a character from one of the artworks and make a list of questions you would like to ask them. Some can be sensible others more fanciful, but make them relevant to your character. When you have between six and ten questions, swap with your partner. Now you have to answer your partner's questions and they have to answer yours. You must pretend to be the character to answer the question. Imagine how they might talk and what attitude they might have to being asked the questions.

The poem can then be made by alternating questions and answers. To indicate that different people are asking and answering, you could use a different typeface or handwriting style. Alternatively, you can make the first verse all the questions and the second verse all the answers. Begin by writing them down as you would speak them, then edit the writing to make it read more as a poem.

The Lady of Shalott, Proserpine or one of the women in 'The Dance' would be good to try this with.

Paint Me a Poem

Make a list of colours in one of the paintings – for example, those in Matisse's 'The Snail'. Now list them down a page with the words 'paint me' in front of each (for example, 'Paint me red').

Now provide a simile that accurately describes that particular shade of the colour and its feeling in the painting. For example, all the colours in 'The Snail' have a jolly, sunny feel to them so you might write:

> Paint me red, like a July sunset.

Repeat this for all the main colours and you will have the makings of a 'paint me' poem. You might have several different tones of the same colour in which case you need a simile for each:

> Paint me red, like a July sunset.

Paint me red, like the fires of hell.

Once you have them all explore what order to put them in to create the best effect. Picasso's paintings 'The Three Dancers' or 'Weeping Woman' would be good inspirations for creating 'paint me' poems.

Six Ways to Look At …

Each person reacts differently to the same piece of music. Some people love hip-hop; others loathe it. In this game, we imagine how different people would react to the same artwork. You need to decide who the six people would be and think how each individual would look at the work.

Let's take Nicholas Hilliard's portrait of Elizabeth I. We will call our poem 'Six Ways to Look at a Queen'. Look at the painting and think of some of the people who would have seen the Queen and how differently each would describe her. We could choose the Queen's hairdresser, her make-up artist, her dressmaker, the gardener who cut the rose she is holding and a prince or ambassador who has come to court her. Begin each verse with 'The Queen is …' – this will help to unify the whole poem. Remember that each person might speak differently: a prince will talk differently to a gardener, for example. Make the final verse how the Queen sees herself. The hairdresser might say:

> The queen is as bald
> As a hard-boiled egg.
> Each day
> When she gets out of bed,
> I hasten to fix
> like a crown on her head
> a glorious curly
> bright red wig.

I hope you make your all your poems dance and sing, paint word pictures and tell stories!

Acknowledgements

My special thanks to Colin Grigg, whose idea it was to introduce the Visual Paths scheme at Tate and who enthusiastically provided the stories and interesting titbits behind the paintings, as well as helping out in the workshops at Tate. He also provided the background notes to all the paintings and pieces of sculpture I was interested in.

My special thanks to all the children who attended the workshops for their fresh responses and exciting contributions to the book, and to the teachers who carried out the follow-up work. The participating schools were: Churchill Gardens Primary, Gloucester Primary, Henry Fawcett Primary, Langdon Primary, Lathom Junior, Marion Richards Primary, Michael Faraday Primary, St Gabriels C of E Primary, Shapla Primary and Vicarage Primary.

Thanks are also due to the Poetry Society who partly funded the residency as part of Poetry Places, and to the sponsors, Morgan Stanley, who supported Colin Grigg's proposal. Finally, thanks to Erin Scapes for her gallery support and to the Visual Paths team of writers and artists who also conducted their own workshops.

Grace Nichols

The Publisher acknowledges the following owners of copyright material used in this book:

Reproductions of all images in this book are © Tate, London, 2004
"Melanie and Me Swimming" by Michael Andrews © the Estate of Michael Andrews
"Maiastra" by Constantin Brancusi © ADAGP, Paris and DACS, London, 2004
"The Fisheater" by Lynn Chadwick © Lynn Chadwick
"Waterfall" by Arshile Gorky © ADAGP, Paris and DACS, London, 2004
"Sea Form (Porthmeor) by Barbara Hepworth © Bowness, Hepworth Estate
"The Snail" by Henri Matisse © Succession H. Matisse/DACS, 2004
"Women and Bird in the Moonlight" by Joan Miro © Successio Miro/DACS, 2004
"The Three Dancers" and "Weeping Woman" by Pablo Picasso © Succession Picasso/DACS, 2004
"The Dance" by Paula Rego © the artist
"Marilyn Diptych" by Andy Warhol © The Andy Warhol Foundation for the Visual Arts, Inc./ARS, NY and DACS, London, 2004